Amanda's Dream
Amandas Traum

Shelley Admont

Illustrated by
Sumana Roy

www.kidkiddos.com
Copyright ©2013 by S.A. Publishing ©2017 by KidKiddos Books Ltd.
support@kidkiddos.com

All rights reserved. No part of this book may be reproduced in any form or by any electronic or mechanical means, including information storage and retrieval systems, without written permission from the publisher, except in the case of a reviewer, who may quote brief passages embodied in critical articles or in a review.
First edition, 2019

Translated from English by Tess Parthum
Aus dem Englischen übersetzt von Tess Parthum
German editing by Veronika Strauss
Deutsche Überarbeitung von Veronika Strauß

Library and Archives Canada Cataloguing in Publication
Amanda´s Dream (English German Bilingual Edition)/ Shelley Admont
ISBN: 978-1-5259-1851-3 paperback
ISBN: 978-1-5259-1852-0 hardcover
ISBN: 978-1-5259-1850-6 eBook

Please note that the German and English versions of the story have been written to be as close as possible. However, in some cases they differ in order to accommodate nuances and fluidity of each language.

There once was a young girl named Amanda. Amanda didn't laugh or smile. She was unhappy.
Es gab einmal ein kleines Mädchen namens Amanda. Amanda lachte oder lächelte nicht. Sie war unglücklich.

Amanda had a lot of friends. She had a loving family and lived in a big house with all the things her heart desired. However, she still felt like something was missing.
Amanda hatte viele Freunde. Sie hatte eine liebevolle Familie und lebte in einem großen Haus mit all den Dingen, die ihr Herz begehrte. Aber sie hatte das Gefühl, dass etwas fehlte.

She didn't smile as she brushed her teeth, combed her hair or even played with her dolls.
Sie lächelte nicht, wenn sie ihre Zähne putzte, ihr Haar kämmte oder sogar mit ihren Puppen spielte.

Every night before bed, she sat with her father and played chess, her favorite game, but it did nothing to cheer her up.
Jeden Abend vor dem Schlafengehen saß sie mit ihrem Vater und spielte ihr Lieblingsspiel Schach, aber es half nicht, sie aufzumuntern.

One day, Amanda was sitting on a bench in the park and reading her favorite book.
Eines Tages saß Amanda auf einer Bank im Park und las ihr Lieblingsbuch.

Out of nowhere, a woman appeared. She wore a beautiful pink dress, and had wavy, flowing locks of hair and big, glowing blue eyes.
Wie aus dem Nichts erschien eine Frau. Sie trug ein wunderschönes, rosafarbenes Kleid und hatte welliges, wallendes Haar und große, leuchtend blaue Augen.

"Hello, Amanda," said the woman as she approached the bench. "Why are you sad?"
„Hallo Amanda", sagte die Frau, als sie sich der Bank näherte. „Warum bist du traurig?"

"I'm not sad," answered Amanda. "I just don't feel like smiling."
„Ich bin nicht traurig", antwortete Amanda. „Mir ist einfach nicht nach Lächeln zumute."

"Are you sure? You seem upset," the strange woman replied.
„Bist du sicher? Du scheinst aufgebracht zu sein", antwortete die fremde Frau.

Amanda decided that she had to talk to someone. She told the woman how unhappy she was. As Amanda breathlessly spilled out all her emotions, she began to cry.

Amanda entschied, dass sie mit jemandem reden musste. Sie erzählte der Frau, wie unglücklich sie war. Als Amanda atemlos all ihre Gefühle nur so aussprudelte, begann sie zu weinen.

Suddenly, Amanda stopped crying, looked at the strange woman and asked, "Who are you and how do you know my name?"
Plötzlich hörte Amanda auf zu weinen, sah die seltsame Frau an und fragte: „Wer bist du und woher kennst du meinen Namen?"

"I'm a dream fairy," the woman said. "I'm here to help you."
„Ich bin eine Traumfee", sagte die Frau. „Ich bin hier, um dir zu helfen."

Amanda listened carefully. "You just need a dream—a goal," the fairy continued.
Amanda hörte aufmerksam zu. „Du brauchst nur einen Traum – ein Ziel", fuhr die Fee fort.

"I know! I really want one. All my friends have a dream," Amanda said with excitement, "and you know what? Their dreams come true."
„Ich weiß! Ich will unbedingt einen. Alle meine Freunde haben einen Traum", sagte Amanda aufgeregt, „und weißt du was? Ihre Träume werden wahr."

"Danny dreamed of riding a bike, and last week he learned to ride all by himself."
„Danny träumte davon, Fahrrad zu fahren, und letzte Woche hat er ganz allein gelernt zu fahren."

"Lillian dreamed of being a ballet dancer, and now she has dance lessons and dances in different shows."
„Lillian träumte davon, Balletttänzerin zu werden, und jetzt hat sie Tanzunterricht und tanzt in verschiedenen Aufführungen."

"I really want to have some kind of dream come true, too. I just don't know how to get one."
„Ich möchte wirklich, dass auch irgendein Traum für mich in Erfüllung geht. Ich weiß nur nicht, wie man einen bekommt."

"A dream isn't something that can be given to you," said the dream fairy. "You need to have one inside your heart. Don't worry, it isn't as hard as it sounds. I can help you."

„Ein Traum ist nichts, was dir gegeben werden kann", sagte die Traumfee. „Du musst einen in deinem Herzen tragen. Keine Sorge, es ist nicht so schwer, wie es klingt. Ich kann dir helfen."

Amanda looked up at her and wiped away her tears. She felt much better now.
Amanda sah zu ihr auf und wischte ihre Tränen weg. Sie fühlte sich jetzt viel besser.

"All you have to do is go home and think about what you want," continued the fairy. "Write down all your favorite things to do and what you love about them."
„Alles, was du tun musst, ist nach Hause zu gehen und darüber nachzudenken, was du möchtest", fuhr die Fee fort. „Schreibe all deine Lieblingsbeschäftigungen auf und was du an ihnen liebst."

After that, she disappeared as if she had never been there at all.
Danach verschwand sie, als wäre sie gar nie dagewesen.

What do I want? I know, I want a lot of candy, thought Amanda on her way home. *No, why do I need a lot of candy? I'll eat a little and then not want any more.*
Was möchte ich? Ich weiß, ich will ganz viele Süßigkeiten, dachte Amanda auf dem Weg nach Hause. Nein, warum brauche ich ganz viele Süßigkeiten? Ich werde ein paar essen und dann keine mehr wollen.

I want a lot of dolls of all different kinds, she thought, but then changed her mind again. *No, I don't need a lot of dolls. I have enough already.*
Ich will ganz viele verschieden Puppen, dachte sie, aber dann änderte sie ihre Meinung wieder. Nein, ich brauche nicht ganz viele Puppen. Ich habe schon genug.

So what do I want? Amanda continued to think hard about what her dream could be. *Maybe a cute little dog?*
„Also, was will ich?", Amanda überlegte angestrengt weiter, was ihr Traum sein könnte. Vielleicht ein süßer, kleiner Hund?

No, it would be better to have new crayons or pretty earrings. Or maybe I want to be a famous actress or a princess?
‚Nein, es wäre besser, neue Buntstifte oder schöne Ohrringe zu haben. Oder vielleicht will ich eine berühmte Schauspielerin oder eine Prinzessin sein?'

She thought of reading her favorite books and of playing with her friends. She thought of music, dancing and painting.
Sie dachte daran, ihre Lieblingsbücher zu lesen mit ihren Freunden zu spielen. Sie dachte an Musik, Tanz und Malerei.

She thought and thought and thought, but she still didn't know what she wanted.
Sie dachte nach und dachte nach und dachte nach, aber sie wusste immer noch nicht, was sie wollte.

She carried on thinking even when her father came home from work. Just like every evening, Amanda and her father played chess.
Sie dachte weiter nach, auch als ihr Vater von der Arbeit nach Hause kam. Wie jeden Abend spielten Amanda und ihr Vater Schach.

She enjoyed playing chess that evening so much that she forgot all about her conversation with the dream fairy.
Sie genoss das Schachspielen an diesem Abend so sehr, dass sie ihr Gespräch mit der Traumfee ganz vergaß.

That night when Amanda went to sleep, she had a dream.
Als Amanda in dieser Nacht schlafen ging, hatte sie einen Traum.

In her dream, she walked through the doors of a big building. She wandered down a long corridor, following the sound of excited voices, until she entered a large room.

In ihrem Traum ging sie durch die Türen eines großen Gebäudes. Sie ging einen langen Korridor hinunter und folgte dem Klang aufgeregter Stimmen, bis sie einen großen Raum betrat.

It was a chess competition. She looked around and heard her name called over the speakers. She was going to play next!
Es war ein Schachwettbewerb. Sie sah sich um und hörte, dass ihr Name über die Lautsprecher aufgerufen wurde. Sie würde als Nächste spielen!

In the first round, Amanda played against children of her own age and won every single match. She was excited, determined and surprisingly good at chess.
In der ersten Runde spielte Amanda gegen Kinder in ihrem Alter und gewann jedes einzelne Spiel. Sie war aufgeregt, entschlossen und erstaunlich gut im Schach.

In the next round, she played against older children and won every match again.
In der nächsten Runde spielte sie gegen ältere Kinder und gewann erneut jedes Spiel.

At the end of the day, she was titled the Chess Champion.
Am Ende des Tages wurde sie zur Schachmeisterin ernannt.

Amanda woke up overjoyed. The dream had felt so real! She wanted to be a chess champion. She picked up a pen, scribbled "chess champion" on a piece of paper and ran out of her room.

Amanda wachte überglücklich auf. Der Traum hatte sich so echt angefühlt! Sie wollte eine Schachmeisterin werden. Sie nahm einen Stift, kritzelte „Schachmeisterin" auf ein Stück Papier und rannte aus ihrem Zimmer.

She hugged her father and shouted, "I'm going to be a chess champion!"
Sie umarmte ihren Vater und rief: „Ich werde eine Schachmeisterin!"

Amanda's father smiled, gave her a tight hug and said, "I believe in you, dear."
Amandas Vater lächelte, drückte sie fest und sagte: „Ich glaube an dich, Liebes."

A few days passed and a chess competition was going to be held at school. There was great excitement in the air.
Ein paar Tage vergingen und in der Schule sollte ein Schachwettbewerb stattfinden. Es lag große Aufregung in der Luft.

Amanda was nervous at first, but she was confident she would win. After all, she had won the championship in her dream.
Amanda war anfangs nervös, aber sie war zuversichtlich, dass sie gewinnen würde. Schließlich hatte sie in ihrem Traum die Meisterschaft gewonnen.

From the moment the competition began, however, it was obvious that Amanda wasn't as strong of a player as she thought. She lost the very first game.
Von dem Moment an, als der Wettbewerb begann, war jedoch klar, dass Amanda nicht so eine starke Spielerin war, wie sie dachte. Sie verlor das allererste Spiel.

She was hurt and disappointed in herself. It wasn't anything like the competition in her dream.
Sie war verletzt und von sich selbst enttäuscht. Es war überhaupt nicht so wie der Wettbewerb in ihrem Traum.

Sad and discouraged, Amanda arrived home. She sat on the bed and started to cry.
Traurig und entmutigt kam Amanda nach Hause. Sie setzte sich auf die Couch und fing an zu weinen.

How could this happen? she thought. *I dreamed about this. I should have won!*
„Wie konnte das passieren?", dachte sie. „Ich habe es doch so geträumt. Ich hätte gewinnen sollen!"

"Why are you crying, dear?" said a familiar voice. The dream fairy was sitting next to her.
„Warum weinst du, Liebes?", sagte eine vertraute Stimme. Die Traumfee saß neben ihr.

"What's the point in having a dream if it doesn't come true?" answered Amanda.
„Was nützt es, einen Traum zu haben, wenn er nicht wahr wird?", antwortete Amanda.

The dream fairy put her arm around Amanda's shoulder. "In order for your dream to come true, you have to practice," she explained kindly. "You have to work hard and try over and over again until you make it happen."
Die Traumfee legte ihren Arm um Amandas Schulter. „Damit dein Traum wahr wird, musst du üben", erklärte sie freundlich. „Du musst hart arbeiten und es immer und immer wieder versuchen, bis du ihn verwirklichst."

Amanda listened carefully to the dream fairy and knew she was right.
Amanda hörte der Traumfee aufmerksam zu und wusste, dass sie recht hatte.

"Do you really, really want to be a chess champion?" asked the fairy.
„Willst du wirklich, wirklich Schachmeisterin sein?", fragte die Fee.

"More than anything else in the world." Amanda smiled and stopped crying.
„Mehr als alles andere auf der Welt." Amanda lächelte und hörte auf zu weinen.

The dream fairy came closer to Amanda and whispered, "Then you know what you should do."
Die Traumfee rückte Amanda näher und flüsterte: „Dann weißt du, was du tun solltest."

Before Amanda could say another word, the fairy disappeared.
Bevor Amanda noch ein Wort sagen konnte, verschwand die Fee.

Amanda thought for a moment, hopped off the bed and ran to her father.
Amanda dachte einen Moment nach, sprang vom Bett und rannte zu ihrem Vater.

"Dad!" she shouted. "I want to be a chess champion!"
„Papa!", rief sie. „Ich will Schachmeisterin sein!"

"I know, Amanda, you've already told me. But how are you going to accomplish it?" he asked.
„Ich weiß, Amanda, du hast es mir schon erzählt. Aber wie willst du das erreichen?", fragte er.

"I want to sign up for a chess club, and I'm going to practice every day. I don't even want to watch TV or play with my toys—I just want to do this."
„Ich möchte mich für einen Schachclub anmelden und ich werde jeden Tag üben. Ich will nicht einmal fernsehen oder mit meinen Spielzeugen spielen – ich will einfach nur das machen."

"Are you sure?" her dad asked.
„Bist du sicher?", fragte ihr Papa.

"Yes!" Amanda answered. "I will do anything to be the chess champion."
„Ja!", antwortete Amanda. „Ich werde alles tun, um Schachmeisterin zu werden."

"I'm proud of you, sweetheart, I know you'll succeed."
„Ich bin stolz auf dich, Schatz, ich weiß, dass du Erfolg haben wirst."

Her father hugged her tightly, and Amanda's face shone with pride and excitement.
Ihr Vater umarmte sie fest und Amandas Gesicht strahlte vor Stolz und Aufregung.

Amanda began to practice for the next competition. She spent most of her days playing chess.
Amanda begann für den nächsten Wettkampf zu trainieren. Sie verbrachte die meisten Tage damit, Schach zu spielen.

She studied at the chess club, practiced on the computer at home and played chess with her dad in the evenings. She didn't mind not playing with her dolls or watching TV—she was focused on becoming the best chess player she could be.
Sie lernte im Schachclub, übte zuhause am Computer und spielte abends Schach mit ihrem Papa. Es störte sie nicht, nicht mit ihren Puppen zu spielen oder fernzusehen – sie war darauf konzentriert, die beste Schachspielerin zu werden, die sie sein konnte.

Finally, the day of the next competition arrived. Amanda excitedly stood up for her first match and met the same boy she had lost to in the previous competition.

Schließlich kam der Tag des nächsten Wettbewerbs. Amanda stellte sich aufgeregt ihrem ersten Spiel und traf auf denselben Jungen, gegen den sie im vorherigen Wettbewerb verloren hatte.

"Are you ready to lose again?" the boy asked mockingly.
„Bist du bereit, wieder zu verlieren?", fragte der Junge spöttisch.

Amanda just smiled. Deep in her heart, she was confident that she was ready.
Amanda lächelte nur. Tief in ihrem Herzen war sie überzeugt, dass sie bereit war.

The match began right away. Amanda won easily and was excited to play more.
Das Spiel begann sofort. Es war so einfach. Amanda gewann mit Leichtigkeit und freute sich darauf, mehr zu spielen.

She won the second match, and the third and the fourth, and on it went. Each match was harder than the one before, but thanks to her hard work and determination, Amanda won every time.
Sie gewann das zweite, dritte und auch vierte Spiel und so ging es immer weiter. Jedes Spiel war schwerer als das Vorherige, aber dank ihrer harten Arbeit und Entschlossenheit gewann Amanda jedes Mal.

At the end of the day, Amanda was awarded the title of School Chess Champion.
Am Ende des Tages wurde Amanda der Titel Schulschachmeisterin verliehen.

She showed her medal and trophy proudly to her family and friends. She was so happy, and knew that she could achieve anything she wanted.

Sie zeigte ihre Medaille und Trophäe stolz ihrer Familie und ihren Freunden. Sie war so glücklich und wusste, dass sie alles erreichen konnte, was sie wollte.

That was how Amanda found her dream and made it come true.
So fand Amanda ihren Traum und verwirklichte ihn.

From that day on, Amanda was never sad again. Now she already knows what her next dream will be and what she has to do to make it come true.
Von diesem Tag an war Amanda nie wieder traurig. Sie weiß schon, was ihr nächster Traum sein wird und was sie tun muss, damit auch dieser in Erfüllung geht.

How about you?
Was ist mit dir?

What's your dream and what will you do to make it come true?
Was ist dein Traum und was wirst du tun, damit er wahr wird?

www.ingramcontent.com/pod-product-compliance
Lightning Source LLC
LaVergne TN
LVHW051933070526
838200LV00077B/4637